Generally speaking an outboard engine will run for as long as it has petrol, air, oil, and electrical power. It is up to you to determine whether you will have to become a permanent mechanic or whether you will be able to enjoy many happy hours of carefree motoring. Stick to the guidelines in the manual, replace the parts that are subject to wear and tear at the right time, and you will not be disappointed in your outboard engine.

The actual buying process is a balancing act between expenditure and environmental awareness. If you are willing to blow about 600 g/kWh of petrol then you should buy a cheap second-hand two stroke engine with carburettor. If, on the other hand, you wish to be more economical you should buy a two or four stroke engine with fuel injection. In most cases that will probably mean halving your fuel consumption.

Example. If you calculate this in absolute figures, it means that at 500 g/kWh with a 37.36 kW (50 hp engine) you will have an hourly fuel consumption of 18.68 kg/h. In litres this works out at 25.94 litres/hour (density 0.72). If you calculate this consumption for a weekend with 4 hours' motoring time it adds up to 104 litres! You can easily calculate what that will cost at current petrol prices. With a fuel injection engine you would spend less than half that and the emissions are also substantially less than with a carburettor engine.

You also need to take into consideration the cruising ground of a boat powered by an outboard engine. There are hardly any that are suitable for oceangoing or even seagoing vessels, in other words boats that would venture out to sea and undertake voyages of 300 miles or more. Hence, when referring to boats powered by outboards, we mean coastal boats which do not solely rely on their own ability to get out of difficulty in an emergency. That means that in an emergency they will receive help and assistance. So go out there and have fun!

▶ *Currently available outboards. Environmental requirements have increased. In 1998 only one company (Honda) had a four stroke engine in its range. Today every brand offers a four stroke engine, with or without fuel injection. The two stroke engines of Evinrude rely on E-Tec. This is a high pressure fuel injection system. Mariner and Mercury have introduced Optimax, also a high pressure fuel injection system but with an Australian patent. For its two stroke engines, Tohatsu has chosen Low Pressure Direct Injection (TLDI). Yamaha also uses a high pressure injection system. Four stroke engines use fuel injection systems like those in car engines.*

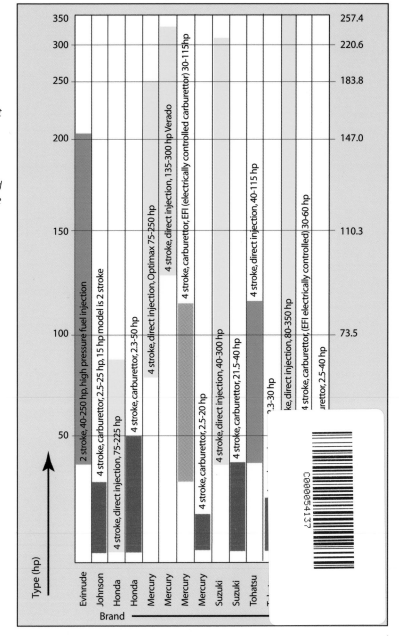

BUYING – MAINTAINING – DRIVING

Outboards are technical sports accessories and as such should be treated with respect. To get the best from your outboard, follow these 3 basic principles:

- Buy the correct engine
- Maintain and service it correctly
- Operate and drive it properly

Buying the correct engine is an undertaking you need to consider very carefully. Ideally, you need to find a dealer who is willing both to mount the engine onto your boat for you and take the time to advise you on how best to use it. This is called delivery service, and in principle it should include the following:

- Most suitable choice of engine
- Appropriate choice of propeller
- Delivery in running condition
- Optimal fuel and ignition tuning
- Testing of gears and steering
- Checking of lubrication, cooling, fuel, electricity and ignition
- Advice on correct operation and use.

If you arrange outboards in order of ease of use, there are 3 categories:

■ Small engines without gears, with built-in fuel tank (max 2 litres) and usually with splash lubrication. These are engines of around 2 kW (2.5 hp) that have to be rotated 180 degrees in order to reverse.

■ Medium-sized engines up to about 40 kW with forward and reverse gears, a separate tank and a rotating handgrip for the accelerator.

■ Large engines from 40 kW upwards which are only suitable for operation by steering wheel and have a single lever for gear and throttle. These engines are too large to be operated manually.

Correct maintenance and servicing requires patience and discipline. Take the time to keep a record of the maintenance plan in a diary or logbook. For an outboard engine the maintenance plan is relatively simple and can be divided into 50 hour (6 monthly) or 100 hour (yearly) running periods. The 50 hour maintenance check should be carried out at some point in the middle of the season, ideally just before the summer holidays, while the 100 hour maintenance check can best be combined with preparing the engine for winter storage.

Operation and driving skills are best developed through accumulated experience. For outboards the motto is: learn by doing but begin by reading all the pages of the user manual. If you also take a look at the following sketches and read the chapter on troubleshooting you are well on your way to carefree motoring.

The most important ground rule is: full speed = nominal rated speed with your trim set at 4 to 6 degrees.

If the engine is behaving abnormally or sounding strange, or if there is no water coming from the control channel, you should bring the revolutions back down or shut off the engine entirely until you have found the problem and solved it.

▶ **1.** *Small, cheap outboards do not have a reverse gear. The engine can be fully rotated and has to be turned through 180 degrees in order to reverse.*

▶ **2.** *Medium sized engines up to approximately 40 kW have a reverse gear and are steered by either a handgrip or a steering wheel.*

▶ **3.** *Larger engines can only be operated by a steering wheel and a single gear lever and throttle.*

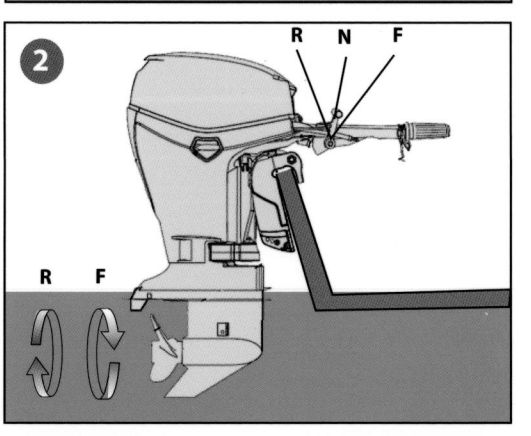

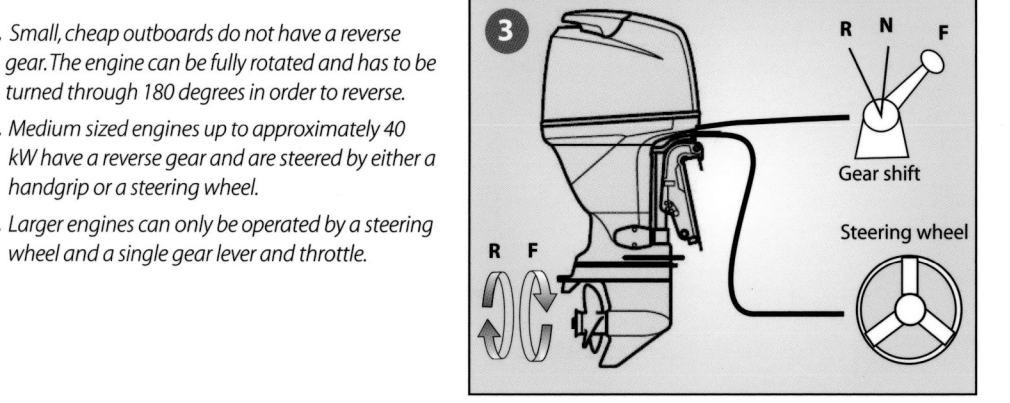

AIR AND FUEL MIX

Outboard engines are available as two or four stroke and with carburettor or fuel injection, although nowadays only small single cylinder engines are fitted with a carburettor.

The advantage of fuel injection is that the injection can be monitored electronically, enabling the outboard to comply with the new stringent environmental regulations. These engines also have a higher turning moment, lower emissions and use less fuel (according to the manufacturers).

There is very little variation between the various manufacturers in the design of the tail, the mounting and the steering system.

The diagrams on this page show the differences in the way air and fuel mixtures are achieved between engines with a carburettor and those with fuel injection.

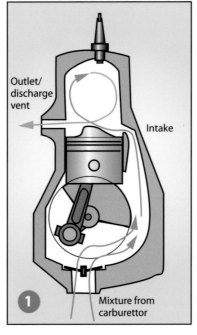

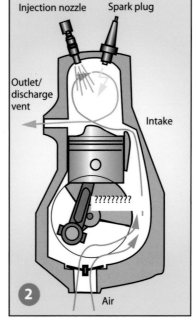

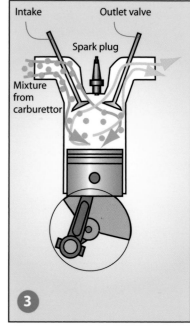

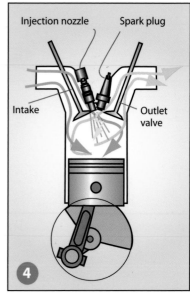

1. *The diagram shows a two stroke engine with air/fuel mixing through a carburettor. These engines are almost obsolete. Their only advantage is that they are cheap. Disadvantages are higher fuel consumption and shorter intervals between services. Due to current fuel prices and stricter environmental requirements no new models of this type are being built.*

2. *Two stroke engine with direct fuel injection. Evinrude now builds this model with a high pressure injection system by Ficht.*

According to statistics from the manufacturer this type is more fuel efficient than a four stroke engine and releases less damaging emissions. The warranty period is 3 years, as is the maintenance interval. Tohatsu has also supplied this type of engine since 2007 but with a low pressure fuel injection system.

3. *The four stroke engine with carburettor is also a thing of the past. It has a high fuel consumption as well as an unacceptable pollution level and a relatively high number of*

parts. This type now exists only as a small one-cylinder engine.

4. *Four stroke engine with direct injection. There are versions with high and low pressure injection. It is not yet clear which of the two is the best. It is a fact, though, that fuel consumption is much lower than that of a carburettor engine and that the emissions are well below legal levels.*

MOUNTING – TRIMMING – PROPELLER

If a professional isn't available to mount and trim your new engine, be aware that this is not an easy task. It's important not to make any mistakes here – the height of the counter of the boat is one of the most critical measurements. Generally speaking the anti-cavitation plate of the engine must be slightly lower in the water than the bottom of the boat. This should not be more than a few centimetres.

Engines above 30 hp are usually attached by fixed bolts. The mounting brackets have 4 to 5 holes allowing the height of the engine to be adjusted. Setting up your boat, engine and propeller correctly requires both care and a certain amount of experience. When planing, the ideal angle of longitudinal heel is between 4 and 6 degrees to the surface of the water.

The weight distribution of the boat should be such that the waterline is parallel to its normal unloaded level. You can then fully open the throttle on a stretch of open water. If the engine reaches its nominal amount of revolutions and the boat is planing at an angle of heel of 4 to 6 degrees, everything has been correctly adjusted and trimmed. If the trim is incorrect and down by the stern the load should be moved forward. You can investigate this by getting one or more passengers to sit further forward. If the result is satisfactory you can then readjust the trim permanently by moving heavy objects such as the tank or other equipment further forward.

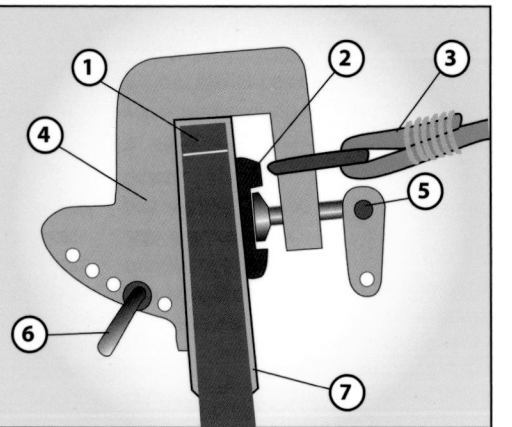

Mounting the engine on the transom
Small to medium engines are attached with transom clamps. (1) height adjustment; (2) clamp plate; (3) safety line; (4) mounting bracket with trim holes; (5) transom clamp; (6) tilt adjustment and (7) metal strengthening of the transom.

▶ *The height of the anti-cavitation plate in relation to the bottom of the boat is an important factor in achieving an efficient and quiet boat. In their manuals some manufacturers advise that this plate and the bottom should be on the same level (1). However, it is advisable to have this plate 2 to 3 centimetres lower in the water to make it less easy for air to travel below the anti-cavitation plate (2). If the plate is mounted higher, the propeller will easily suck in air causing it to run free and cavitate (3).*

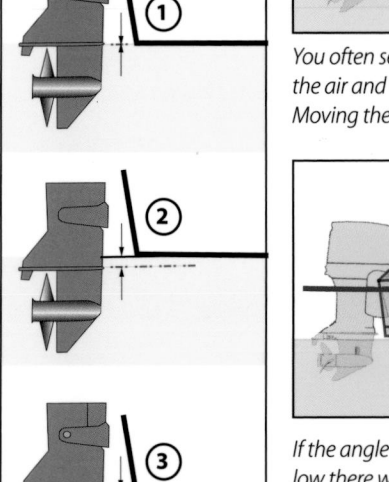

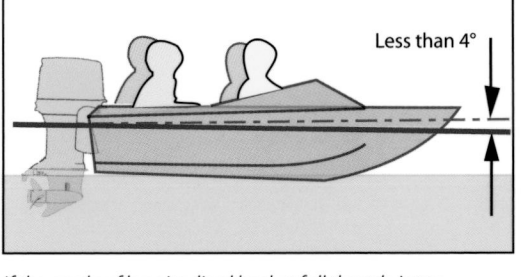

4– 6°

The ideal vertical angle for planing is between 4 and 6 degrees. If the engine reaches its optimum number of revolutions, you have chosen the correct propeller.

More than 6°

You often see boats planing with their bow too high up in the air and their stern being sucked down into the water. Moving the centre of gravity forward will correct this

Less than 4°

If the angle of longitudinal heel at full throttle is too low there will be too much friction between hull and water, causing fuel consumption to rise. Altering the tilt adjustment of the mounting bracket can improve this.

CHECKS BEFORE STARTING

Engines need regular attention, and a responsible skipper will take 2 or 3 minutes to check the condition of his engine before starting it. All the systems that enable the engine to run smoothly must be working properly. In order of importance they are: fuel, lubrication, electricity and cooling.

Two stroke engines

With two stroke engines the correct oil/fuel mix is of crucial importance and it should be part of your daily routine to check the level in the oil reservoir.

▶ Engine checklist before and after use

Don't be alarmed when you read: 'check filter'. This doesn't mean that the filter needs to be dismantled, but simply visually checked for leakage or the presence of water. Carrying out tasks from the maintenance list will be dealt with in a later chapter. Once a day open the hood and check for leakage and for any parts that may have become loose due to vibration. You should also repeat this visual check after a trip. If you identify a problem it can be dealt with before the next trip or after the engine has been taken to a workshop.

CHECKS TO MAKE BEFORE A TRIP

Check for loose parts, wear and tear and leaks. If you see any abnormalities you must resolve them before you leave. These checks should be carried out before the engine is started:

Engine hood	Remove
Fuel system	Check hoses, filters and their attachments for leaks. The priming valve must be squeezed two or three times until resistance is felt.
Tank	Is there enough fuel for the proposed trip?
Mixture	Is the mixture correctly adjusted?
Oil	Is there enough oil on board?
Electricity	Inspect the cables, ignition coil, spark plugs; is the insulation in order and are there any loose cables?
Steering	Emergency switch: Remove it and attach it again. Steering: Does the engine rotate easily? Throttle: Does the mechanism move easily when the throttle is moved? Choke: Does the choke mechanism move properly when the choke is adjusted?
Hand starter	Pull gently on the starter cord and listen for the starter mechanism engaging.
Clutch	Move the handle and listen for the gear change.
Tail fin	Tilt the engine forward and inspect the propeller (fishing line, plastic bag, damage?). Are the anodes in order? Lower the engine back down again.
Miscellaneous	Are the transom clamps properly attached? Is the safety line properly attached? Are there spare parts on board?

You can now replace and lock the engine hood. If everything is satisfactory you can start the engine.

STARTING THE ENGINE

Don't start the engine until you have read this page. Starting an engine is a straightforward procedure and a matter of following a simple routine. For hand starting there are 5 preparatory steps that you need to follow:

1. Place the gear shift in neutral
2. Pump the priming valve
3. Attach the emergency stop cord
4. Put the throttle in 'start' mode
5. Pull out the choke handle.

Starting: for hand starting see the 5 steps set out on the right. When using the hand pull cord remember that you need enough space behind you. Once the engine is running check immediately that there is sufficient cooling water coming from the back of the engine.

Always run the engine for 1 or 2 minutes without putting it into gear. Listen to whether the engine is running smoothly. Only after this should you leave the dock.

Important: do not drive at full throttle for the first 5 to 10 minutes; run the engine at half speed at the most until it has warmed up. Even then you should try to avoid driving at full throttle: generally speaking 80% revs should be the maximum. That is better for the engine, the environment and your purse.

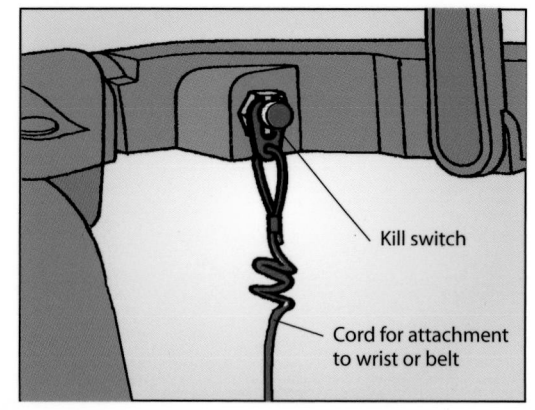

Kill switch

Cord for attachment to wrist or belt

The following 5 steps should be the normal procedure when starting an engine by hand:

1. Look behind you to see if you have sufficient space (at least 80 cm) to pull the starting cord.

2. Lock the tilt adjustment*. Steady yourself with one hand on the engine hood while you pull the starting cord with the other. This will counteract the reaction forces when the engine starts.

3. Now slowly pull the cord till you feel pressure. The starting mechanism is in contact with the flywheel.

4. Pull strongly and smoothly, so that the engine makes the required revolutions.

5. Slowly release the cord so it rewinds itself properly. If the engine does not start immediately repeat the procedure. If the engine still does not start you will need to try to find the cause (see page 15 for checklist).

*If the tilt adjustment isn't locked, the engine will shoot upwards as soon as it is put into reverse gear. After starting, decide whether to leave it locked or release it in order to protect the propeller and the tail fin when in shallow water.

5. Slowly let rope recoil

4. Pull powerfully (start) **3.** Tension cord

1. At least 80 cm space

2. Block tilt mechanism

Full throttle

Slow
Start
Change gear

Indicator for the position of the throttle on the handgrip

◄ The kill switch is a safety precaution to ensure that the engine stops if the helmsman is too far away from it (for instance if he falls overboard). The line pulls the clip out from under the kill switch, disabling the ignition. Every engine should have this device and you should always use it.

▲ The hand starter will remain in good condition if it is not used in an uncontrolled manner. It is important to follow carefully the 5 steps as described.

CARE AND MAINTENANCE

The purpose of maintenance is to prevent problems occurring. Most maintenance jobs can be carried out with relatively simple tools and a reasonable skill level. If, on the other hand, you wish the maintenance to be carried out professionally, you need to go to a reliable workshop. Looking after your engine should result in it starting reliably, running smoothly and having a long life.

The maintenance plan shown on the right is typical. Some manufacturers halve the maintenance periods if the engine is used in salt water. My advice is to carefully follow the list 'Checks to make before a trip' (see page 6) and act immediately if something is wrong. Of course, you should not neglect those less frequent tasks such as replacing oil and filters.

A TYPICAL MAINTENANCE PLAN

There are some misconceptions about the maintenance needed after the first 10 hours of motoring. This maintenance is only necessary until the engine has been run in. After that, maintenance at longer intervals, such as in spring and winter, are enough. Strictly follow the maintenance guidelines given by the manufacturer. The items marked with an asterisk are dependant on the type of engine (for example, 'valve clearance' only applies to a four stroke: a two stroke will not normally have valves).

MAINTENANCE PLAN

This is a typical plan based on information supplied by various manufacturers. The maintenance periods can be seen as technically standard.
- Can be done by the owner
- Has to be done by a workshop

Engine part	Maintenance	Running in period — After 10 hours	After 50 hours, or every 3 months	After 100 hours, or every 6 months	After 200, hours or every year	Page reference
Spark plugs	Clean	●	if necessary ●			9.1
Spark plugs	Check gap	●			●	9.2
Battery	Test/refill	●			●	9.3
Battery	Test	●			●	10.1
Starter motor	Test	●●			●●	10.2
Starting cord	Test	●	●		●	9.4
Lubrication points	Lubricate	●	●		●	9.5
Fuel hoses	Test (leakage)	●	●		●	9.6
Fuel filter	Clean	●	●		●	10.4
Lubrication oil	Check/refresh	●	●		●	10.5
Carburettor	Clean	●●	if necessary		●●	10.6
Stationary revs	Set	●●	if necessary		●●	11.1
Engine block and tail fin	Check (corrosion)	●	●		●	11.2
Cooling system	Flush (fresh water)	●	●		●	11.3
Propeller	Test (split pin)	●	●		●	12.1
Tail fin	Check	●	●		●	11.2
Cool water pump	Test	●	●		●●	11.5
Thermostat	Test				●●	11.4
Oil in tail fin	Change	●	●		●	12.2
Lubrication oil (4 stroke)*	Change	●	●		●	12.3
Moving parts	Lubricate/grease	●	●		●	9.5
Trim and tilt system	Check oil and flap	●	●		●	9.5
Lubrication oil tank	Leakage/damage/filter	●	●		●	12.3
Valve clearance*	Check/set	●●	if necessary		●●	12.5
Anodes (outside)	Test/replace	●	●		●	12.4
Anodes (inside)	Test/replace	●●	●		●	12.4

MAINTENANCE

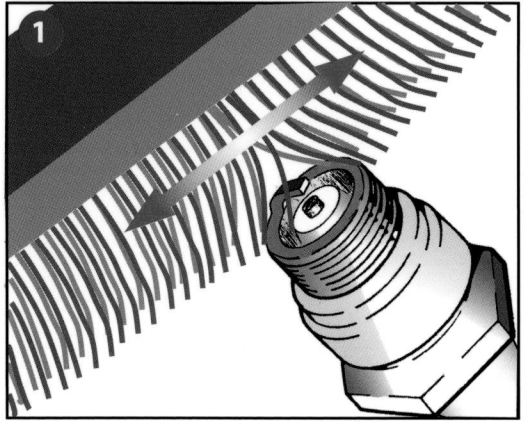

1. With use, spark plugs gradually become dirty. Depending on the type of fuel you use, layers of soot and other pollution build up on the spark plugs and you should clean them periodically with a steel brush. Depending on the level of contamination, the spark will become less powerful.

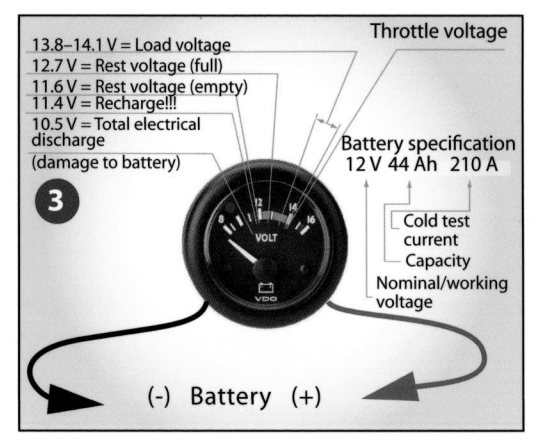

13.8–14.1 V = Load voltage
12.7 V = Rest voltage (full)
11.6 V = Rest voltage (empty)
11.4 V = Recharge!!!
10.5 V = Total electrical discharge (damage to battery)

Throttle voltage

Battery specification 12 V 44 Ah 210 A

Cold test current
Capacity
Nominal/working voltage

(-) Battery (+)

3. The battery charge level is a good general indicator of the capacity of the battery. This diagram gives the values for a lead-acid battery. You can measure the capacity more accurately by using a hydrometer, which measures the density of the battery acid.

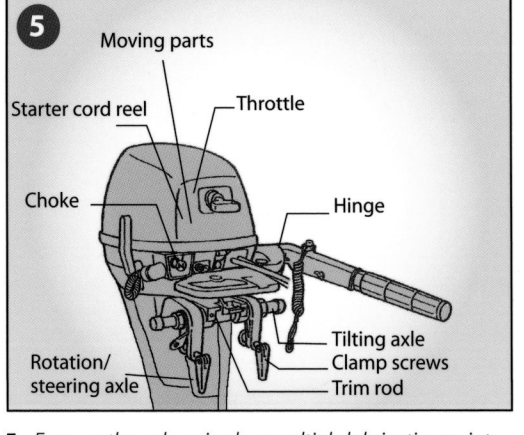

Moving parts
Starter cord reel
Throttle
Choke
Hinge
Rotation/ steering axle
Tilting axle
Clamp screws
Trim rod

5. Every outboard engine has multiple lubrication points that you should grease on a regular basis – the points on the axels are the most important. There will be a detailed diagram in your manufacturer's maintenance manual.

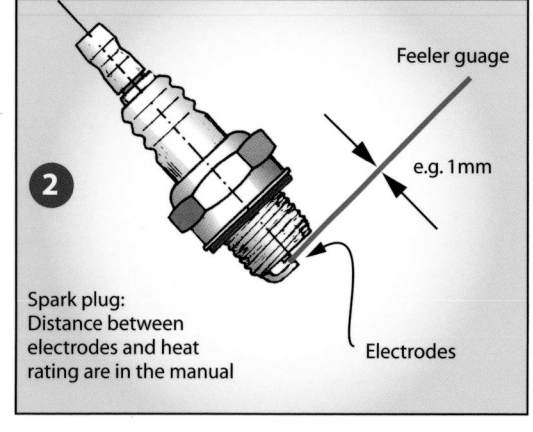

Feeler guage
e.g. 1mm
Spark plug:
Distance between electrodes and heat rating are in the manual
Electrodes

2. You can find the distances between the spark plug electrodes in the manual. Every once in a while they should be checked using a feeler gauge. By carefully bending the outside electrode you can fine-tune the gap.

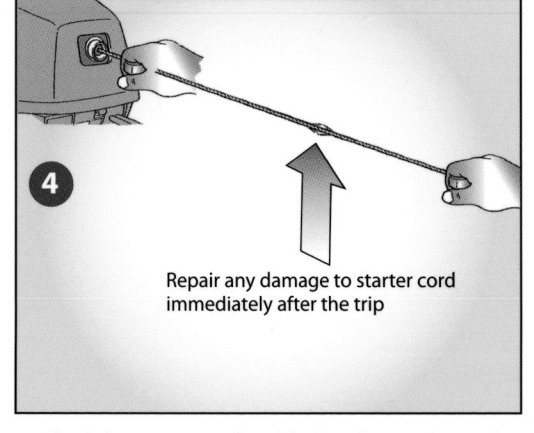

Repair any damage to starter cord immediately after the trip

4. Check the starting cord and the handle attachment for wear and tear once a year. If the cord or handle breaks and the spring is pulled inside the hood you will have to deal with a difficult repair.

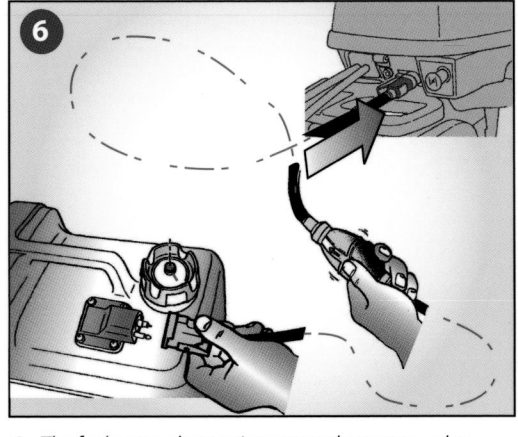

6. The fuel system has various parts that you need to maintain properly. Look carefully at all the couplings between the tank and carburettor or injection pump. Checking for leaks is important as leaking petrol means risk of fire or explosion.

MAINTENANCE

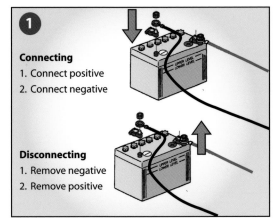

Connecting
1. Connect positive
2. Connect negative

Disconnecting
1. Remove negative
2. Remove positive

1. *Connecting or disconnecting the battery clamps in the wrong order can damage the electronic components of the engine. When connecting, attach the positive clamp first and then the negative. When disconnecting the system, remove the negative clamp first and then the positive.*

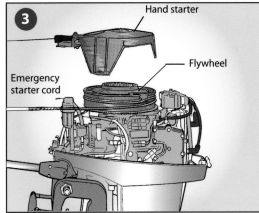

3. *If the hand starter cord is broken you can use an emergency cord to start the engine. Depending on the type of engine, dismantle the hand starter, attach an emergency cord around the flywheel and start the engine with this.*

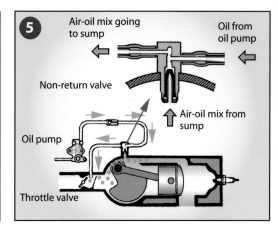

5. *Two stroke engines do not have an oil sump like four stroke engines do; lubricating oil is mixed with the fuel or added through a dosing pump. The pump squeezes the oil from the oil tank through a mixing valve to the carburettor, where it is mixed with the air that is sucked in here.*

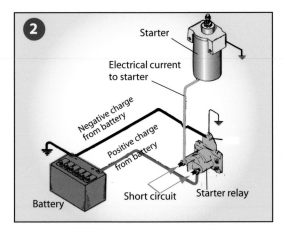

2. *Starter relay. The electrical supply current (red) runs from the battery to the starter relay and (black) to the earth attachment of the engine. A thick cable (orange) runs from the starter relay to the starter. If the starter relay doesn't work it can be short-circuited by using a screwdriver (green).*

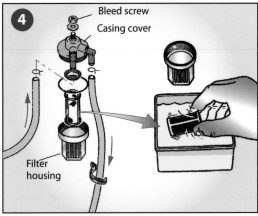

4. *Open and clean the fine filter in the fuel supply hose in case water, air or sediment have accumulated here. Cleaning it is an easy operation: simply wash the metal filter in clean petrol and replace the paper filter.*

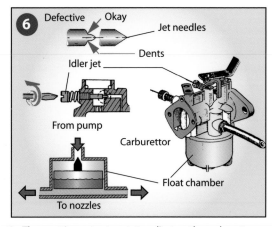

6. *The most important parts to adjust on the carburettor are the fuel jets. The jets will close properly as long as there are no chips or dents. If you cannot regulate the stationary jets and clean the float chamber yourself you should take the carburettor to a workshop for servicing.*

MAINTENANCE

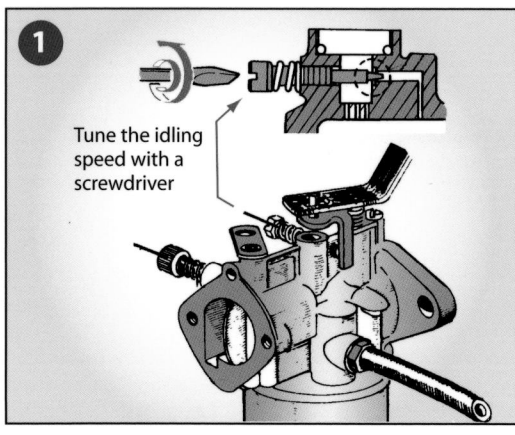

1. Tune the idling speed with a screwdriver

1. *The idling RPM is the basic RPM of the engine. If you set it too high the engine will waste fuel. If you set it too low the engine will stall. Tuning the idling speed is therefore very important. You should keep to the factory setting as much as possible.*

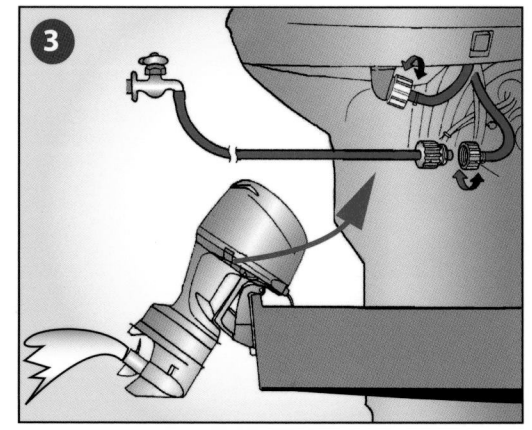

3. *Manufacturers advise rinsing an engine with fresh water after use in salt water. This is especially important for the aluminium parts. Many engines have an attachment to facilitate easy flushing. However, you shouldn't overdo it: once every two weeks should be enough.*

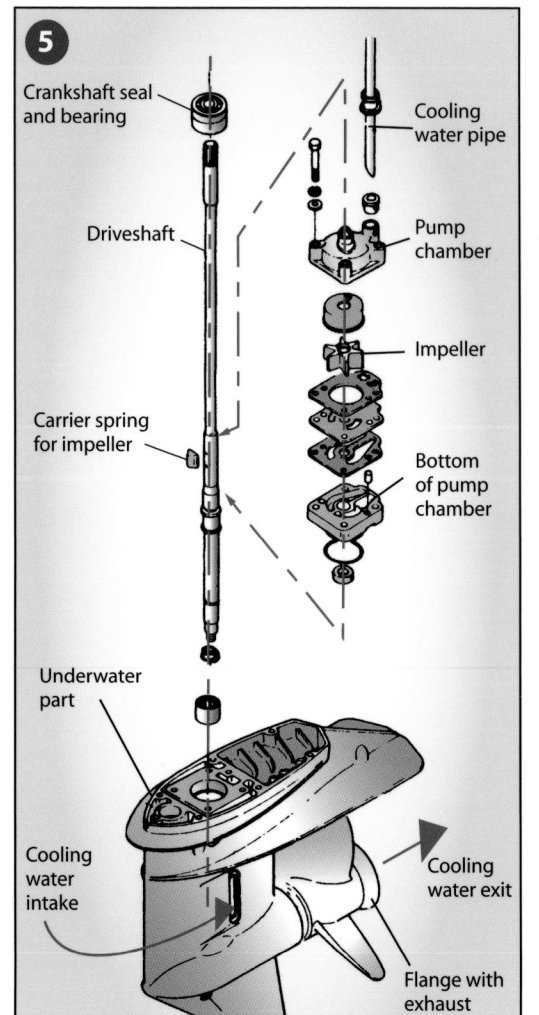

Crankshaft seal and bearing

Cooling water pipe

Driveshaft

Pump chamber

Impeller

Carrier spring for impeller

Bottom of pump chamber

Underwater part

Cooling water intake

Cooling water exit

Flange with exhaust

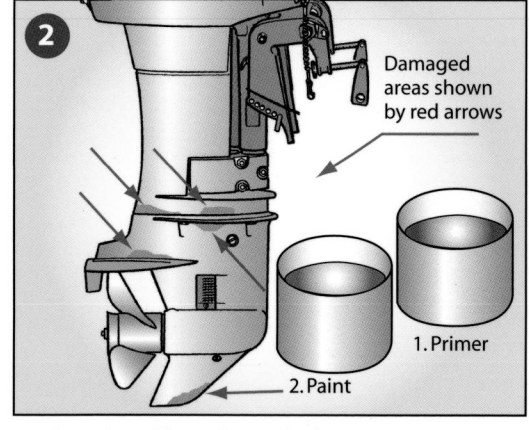

Damaged areas shown by red arrows

1. Primer
2. Paint

2. *Clean the tail fin and propeller thoroughly at least once a year. Any damage can then be repaired. As many parts are made of aluminium, use a special primer to get the best bonding.*

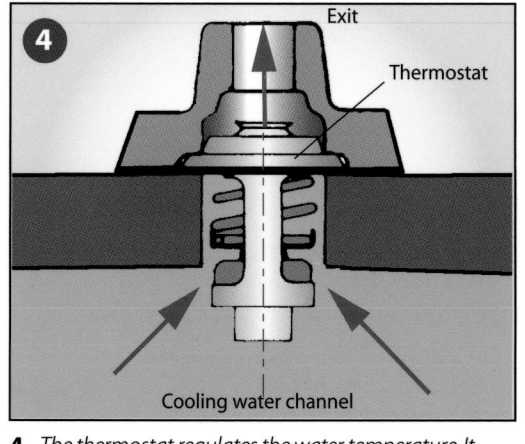

Exit

Thermostat

Cooling water channel

4. *The thermostat regulates the water temperature. It shuts down after the engine starts running so that the engine block warms up more quickly. Once the running temperature has been reached it will automatically open. Thermostats seldom malfunction but if yours does you should repair or replace it.*

5. *The cooling pump is an impeller attached to the driveshaft. If you don't have experience in this area you should ask a workshop to carry out any maintenance. The impeller should be inspected and possibly replaced once every two years. Proper cooling prevents undue wear and tear to the engine.*

11

MAINTENANCE

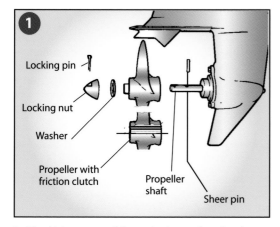

1. The driving power of the engine is transferred to the propeller via a friction clutch sheer pin. Both parts are there for safety reasons. Treat both of them with water-resistant grease at least once a year to prevent the propeller from jamming on the shaft.

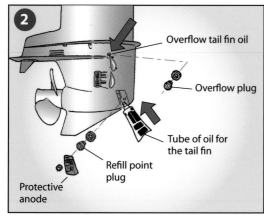

2. The reversing clutch is at the bottom of the tail fin. You should replace the oil in here every year. For this you have to remove the overflow plug and the plug from the refill point and collect the old oil. The new oil is squeezed into the refill point until it overflows.

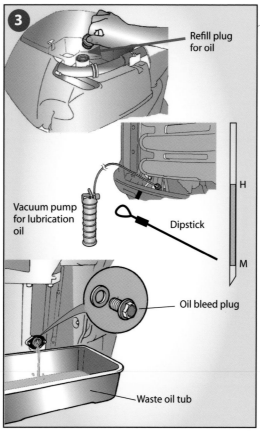

3. Four stroke engines need lubrication oil; the refill plug is on top of the engine block. The oil collects in the sump and is pumped through the channels to the various lubrication points. The draw-off plug is usually inside the housing of the driveshaft. You can also suck up the oil with a vacuum pump through the dipstick opening and save yourself the bother of dismantling the outer cover. There are marks on the dipstick denoting the maximum and minimum levels. Replacing the oil should be done while the engine is warm or the old oil will be too thick and therefore difficult to remove.

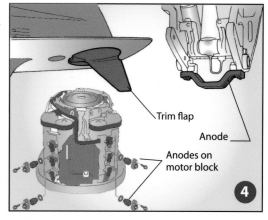

4. If you prepare the engine for winter storage yourself it is important to check the anodes and to replace those that are worn. One anode is attached to the bottom of the anti-cavitation plate as a trim vane. Another will be close to the transom mount while several smaller ones will be attached to the engine block as bolts.

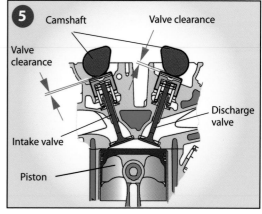

5. Modern four stroke engine valves are driven directly by the camshaft. The valve clearance is set by the manufacturer and can be checked using a feeler gauge when the valve is completely shut.

WINTERIZING

Preparing an engine for winter storage is one of the most important maintenance tasks. Doing this properly should guarantee long and problem-free use of your engine. Only prepare an engine for the winter yourself if it has been running properly during the season and there has been no loss of power (see page 25) or need for repairs. If this is not the case, or if you do not enjoy tinkering with your engine, then you are better off taking it to a workshop.

Welded from steel bars   Screwed wood

▲ *You should remove the engine from the boat for the winter. It's a good idea to use a custom-made transport cart for transporting your engine. It will also make maintenance work much easier. The cart must be fitted with a strong cross beam: bolt the engine to this. You could also make a dust cover, but this must be fully ventilated, otherwise condensation will develop and cause corrosion.*

WINTER STORAGE

WINTERIZING– BY A WORKSHOP

Tasks to be carried out by a workshop when preparing an engine for the winter:

Two stroke engines

- Test run in a test tank and measure the RPMs
- Flush the cooling system
- Test start by hand and/or electrically
- Measure the ignition with an RPM test
- Test the carburettor or injectors
- Test and then clean the spark plugs
- Test the water pump and flush the cooling system
- Test the fuel pump
- Test and clean the thermostat
- Test the gears and bearings
- Drain and replace the oil in the tail fin
- Check the propeller shaft and gaskets
- Lubricate the engine according to the plan in the manual
- Test and clean the tank
- Final test run in test tank followed by storage

Four stroke engines – additional tasks

- Test and tune valve clearance
- Check the drive belt and camshaft
- Change the lubricating oil and filters

WINTER STORAGE

WINTERIZING– DOING IT YOURSELF

- Build or buy a transport and storage cart
- Rinse the engine with fresh water (see page 11 diagram 3)
- Clean and oil the tail fin (see page 12 diagrams 1 and 2)
- Clean the outside of the engine (see page 11 diagram 2)
- Clean the fuel system (see page 10 diagram 4)
- Check nuts and bolts to see if they have loosened due to vibration; remove any corrosion (see page 9 diagram 5)
- Test and clean the electrical system and spark plugs (see page 9 diagrams 1 and 2)
- Drain and replace the oil in the tail fin
- Rotate the flywheel a half turn every 14 days to ensure the oil layer remains. Ideally, the engine should be stored in a semi-heated space. (See drawing below.)

Four stroke engines – additional tasks

- Test and tune valve clearance
- Check the drive belt and camshaft
- Change the lubricating oil and filters

Condensation and combustion residue

Spray some oil in the cylinders after removing the spark plugs, and rotate the flywheel a half turn every two to four weeks to prevent condensation and combustion residue forming on the piston and the piston ring.

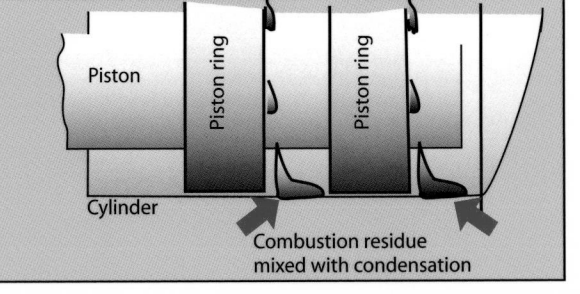

Piston

Piston ring

Piston ring

Cylinder

Combustion residue mixed with condensation

ANALYZING AND REPAIRING MALFUNCTIONS

An outboard engine is designed to run smoothly as long as it receives the correct mix of air and fuel in its cylinder and the spark plugs produce a spark. Therefore, the fuel supply and the ignition are the first systems to look at when troubleshooting. Correct lubrication and cooling are equally important, so there are four main systems that have to be in good working order for an engine to run smoothly. You can become aware of malfunctions either through alarm signals or unusual readings from the instruments.

Troubleshooting flowcharts can make it possible to search systematically for the cause of a problem. They can provide answers to difficult questions and can help you to resolve malfunctions more effectively. The chart below gives an overview of some possible problems that could be solved using logical thinking and deduction. The overall symptom is outlined (for instance 'Engine doesn't start'); you then refer to the appropriate page for further detail.

Obvious problems

The fuel tank is empty

The bleeder screw in the tank lid is shut

Fuel has not been pumped up with the priming valve

There is no cooling water

The battery master switch is not switched on

The battery is flat

The engine fuse is faulty

General malfunctions	Page
Engine doesn't start	14/15
Engine starts but doesn't run properly	16
Engine stalls when throttle is opened up	16
No telltale spout of cooling water	17
Power decreases suddenly	18
Power decreases gradually	18
Bad transition from stationary to higher revs and/or not enough revs when at full throttle	19
Engine stalls after short period of running	20
Engine smokes and runs irregularly	21
Engine runs but boat doesn't reach hull speed	21
Boat doesn't reach maximum hull speed	21
Boat reaches hull speed but engine revs increase without boat accelerating	21
Emergency repairs	22
Engine runs irregularly when idling	23
Engine vibrates	23
Engine has fallen overboard	24

▶ *Sometimes with an electronic ignition the insulation can't withstand the 30,000 V and the system shorts. You should therefore grip the cable with an insulated pair of pliers.*

◀ *If the engine malfunctions you can find the cause by using this checklist.*

ANALYZING A MALFUNCTION

ENGINE DOESN'T START

Whatever the type of engine or ignition, always check the ignition and the fuel system first. If you don't find problems there, you should then look at the electrical system and air/fuel mix.

Hand start

1. Do the spark plugs give a powerful spark?

↓   ↓

YES   NO (see page 9 diagram 1)

↓

Unscrew each spark plug, hold it against the negative earth and run the engine.

Hold the spark plug cable with insulated pliers

2. Is there enough fuel entering the cylinder?

↓   ↓

YES   NO (see page 10 diagram 4)

FUEL SYSTEMS

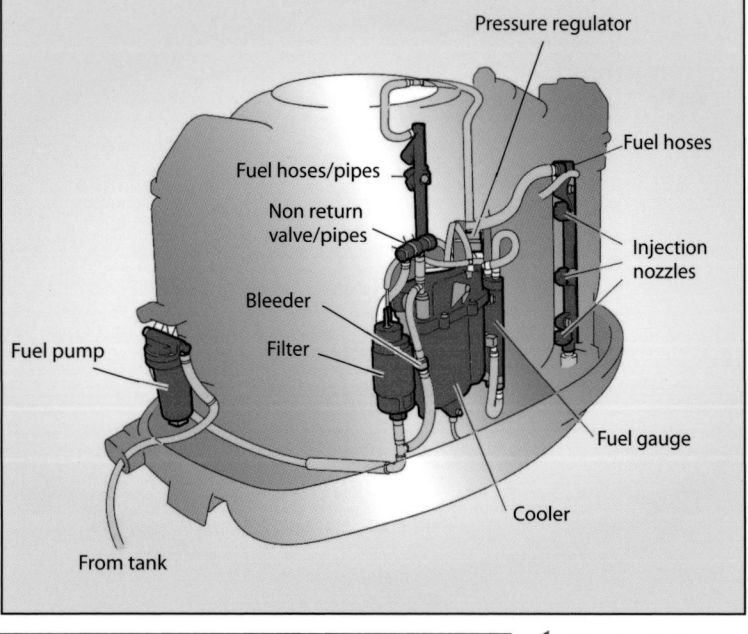

Pressure regulator
Fuel hoses
Fuel hoses/pipes
Non return valve/pipes
Injection nozzles
Bleeder
Filter
Fuel pump
Fuel gauge
Cooler
From tank

◀ *This diagram shows a four stroke engine with low pressure injection. Behind the fuel connection you can see the fuel pump. From here, the fuel runs through a filter and then via a non-return valve to the cooler. From there the fuel passes through the bleeder and the pressure regulator to finally reach the injection nozzles through the distributor. If the system malfunctions the first place to look is the filter. (Clean it.)*

ANALYZING THE MALFUNCTION

ENGINE DOESN'T START

What you need for trouble free starting:

- Enough fuel in the tank
- Fuel hose connected
- No kink in the cable
- Pump valve pressurized
- Choke pulled out
- If the choke is pulled out but the engine is warm the engine will flood.
- If this happens, close the choke and restart the engine several times.

If all these conditions have been met and the engine still doesn't start, check the following:

→ **1.** The ignition
→ **2.** The fuel

1. Are all the cable plugs connected properly? (Check the plugs, especially the spark plugs, and the ignition coil.)

→ Start → No success?
→ Remove and check the spark plugs (see page 16).

If the spark plugs are in order:

→ Replace → Start → No success?
→ Check the fuel systems!
(See diagram to the left.)

2. Loosen the fuel connection. Does fuel come from the hose when you pump the pump valve? If not, look at the tank. If you can't find any problem here then check:

- the choke (see diagram on page 17)
- the throttle valve (see diagram page 17)
  → Start → No success? → Workshop!

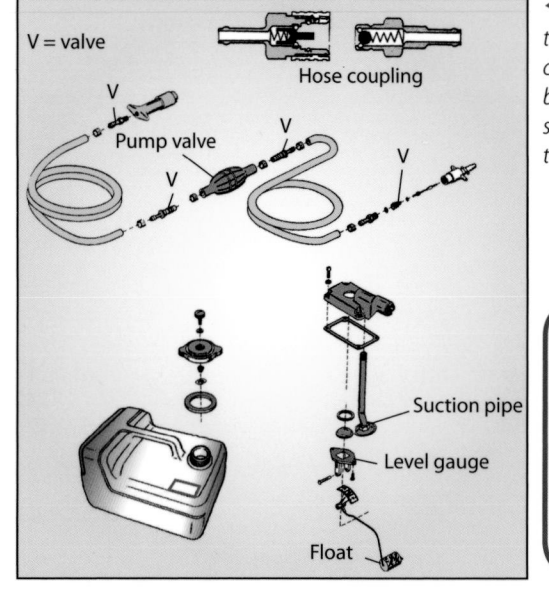

V = valve
Hose coupling
V
Pump valve
V
V
V
Suction pipe
Level gauge
Float

◀ *All engine fuel systems are quite similar. Ensure that there are no leaks and that the valves (V) function correctly. Pump the pump valve for as long as it takes to build up pressure. The system is now primed with fuel. It is standard practice to clean the suction pipe every two or three years and replace the gasket.*

Beware! Rotating parts!

When running the engine with the hood open you must be extremely careful with the moving parts such as the flywheel. With many engines the gear ring is not covered so take great care. A sleeve can easily get caught and lead to serious injury.

WHAT DO YOUR SPARK PLUGS LOOK LIKE?

Colour: red to yellow, brown or grey.
Combustion residue: hardly any.
Electrodes: not charred.
Spark plugs are in good working order.
The engine is correctly tuned.

Colour: dark brown.
Combustion residue: moist, dirty and sooty.
Causes: driving too slowly; the carburettor is delivering a mixture that contains
too much oil (idling adjustment); there is too much oil in the fuel; the mixing system is not working correctly; the contact breaker contacts are worn out; the ignition tension is too low; you have the wrong spark plugs (the heat value is too high).

Colour: white to grey.
Combustion residue: blistering.
Causes: the ignition is too early; there is not enough cooling water (the impeller is broken); the cooling system is blocked
with dirt, scale or salt; there is air or a poor mix in the carburettor; you have the wrong spark plugs (the heat value is too high); the piston rings are stuck. Take your engine to a workshop.

Colour: metallic grey.
Combustion residue: grainy and stuck fast.
Causes: the ignition is too early because the insulation is too hot (you have the wrong spark plugs). If this is the case the
power will also decrease sharply. This is very unusual if the correct spark plugs have been fitted. After replacing the spark plugs you should not use the engine before a thorough check has been carried out in the workshop.

Combustion residue: the electrodes are joined together by accumulated residue and have short-circuited.
Cause: see below.

Bridges around the central electrode.
Combustion residue: grainy, often with *glass blisters and ash.*
Causes: combustion residue has accumulated and become charcoal
(caused by bad oil or too much oil in the fuel); using full throttle immediately after motoring slowly.

Setting the correct distance between the electrodes is important in order to create a good spark. You can use a feeler gauge to determine this distance. You can then adjust the distance by carefully bending the electrode. The correct distance is given in the manual.

Spark plug with ring electrode and multiple electrodes

In theory a spark plug with ring electrodes is the same as a normal spark plug. The difference is that the electrode doesn't project past the end of the plug and doesn't cover the central electrode. Engines
and spark plugs are tuned to each other so you can only use spark plugs that are specified by the manufacturer; using the wrong spark plugs can damage the engine. Bad starting is only the beginning of your problems!

ANALYZING THE MALFUNCTION

ENGINE STARTS BUT DOESN'T RUN PROPERLY – IGNITION IS IRREGULAR

Single or multiple cylinder engines

Test spark plug   → See left and page 9 diagram 1

Moment of ignition has changed
Test synchronisation   → Workshop
Check moment of ignition   → Workshop
Flywheel pin has sheered   → Workshop
(not easily seen with most engines)

Multiple cylinder engines

Spark plug cables have been swapped   → Rectify

ENGINE STALLS WHEN THROTTLE IS OPENED UP

Idling speed is incorrect

Propeller jammed by rubbish.
Clear propeller and try again.
Other causes: tail fin is damaged;
collision damage;
wear and tear;
damaged parts?   → Workshop

When engine is put into gear the increased load is enough to stop the engine

The idling RPM is set too low
or the fuel and oil mix is incorrect
(see pages 17 and 19).   → Workshop

THE COOLING SYSTEM

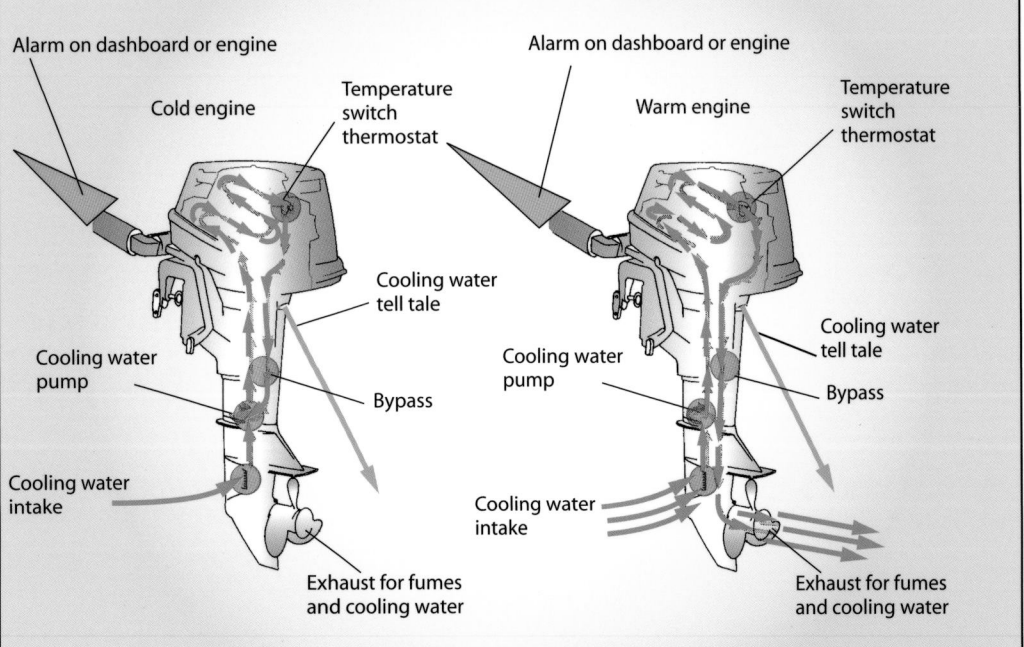

- Alarm on dashboard or engine
- Cold engine
- Temperature switch thermostat
- Cooling water tell tale
- Cooling water pump
- Bypass
- Cooling water intake
- Exhaust for fumes and cooling water

- Alarm on dashboard or engine
- Warm engine
- Temperature switch thermostat
- Cooling water tell tale
- Cooling water pump
- Bypass
- Cooling water intake
- Exhaust for fumes and cooling water

▲ *Diagram of the cooling system – simplified for clarity. Once the engine has reached its working temperature the cooling water will run through the engine block via the opened thermostat. Until the working temperature is reached the cooling water runs through a channel back to the engine.*

▶ *On the right is a sectional plan of a carburettor. First the air flows past the choke valve and then past the carburettor and the throttle valve. The fuel flow is regulated by the float so as not to flood the carburettor. Two important functions are drawn and described: starting and idling.*

- *Starting: The choke and throttle valve are closed. When the engine is started, a vacuum is created behind the valves that sucks air through the carburettor. The air flows past the valves and via the short circuit channel where extra air is sucked in from the starting air intake. This air current sucks a proportionally large amount of fuel in through the carburettor delivering an extra rich mix to the cylinder. When the engine is started and the choke is pushed in the engine will settle into idling mode.*

- *Idling mode: The choke is opened and the air can enter through the open channel. The throttle valve is still shut so the air is led via the short circuit channel past the idling valve. The engine receives the idling fuel/air mix.*

ANALYZING THE MALFUNCTION

NO COOLING WATER

In the case of engines with a cooling water warning system through a thermometer, a pressure gauge or an overheating protector, you can often find the problem in the warning system (for instance, it might have short circuited due to a worn cable).

If no water is coming from the control opening, the following may solve the problem:

- Hinge the engine forward and check the cooling water intake
- Check with a piece of wire whether the opening is blocked
- Check the thermostat (see page 11)
- If the cooling water pump is faulty, take it to a workshop
- If the water channel in the engine is blocked, take it to a workshop

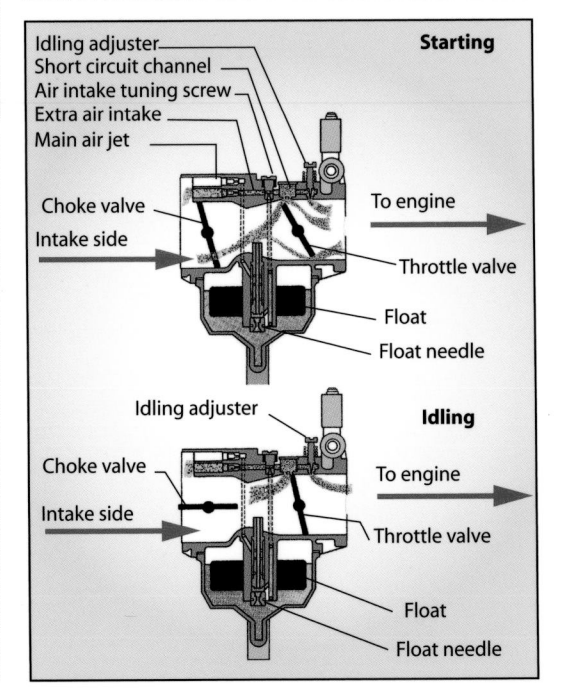

Starting
- Idling adjuster
- Short circuit channel
- Air intake tuning screw
- Extra air intake
- Main air jet
- Choke valve
- Intake side
- To engine
- Throttle valve
- Float
- Float needle

Idling
- Idling adjuster
- Choke valve
- Intake side
- To engine
- Throttle valve
- Float
- Float needle

PROPELLER SHAFT DEFECTS

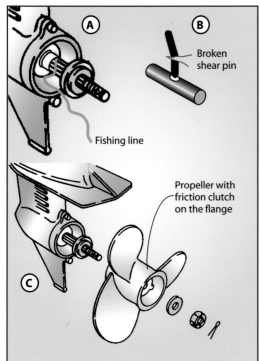

FILTER MAINTENANCE

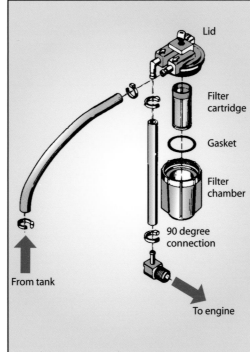

POWER DECREASES SUDDENLY

Stop the engine and raise it!

Something like a rope or plastic bag has probably got tangled in the propeller.

If you think that the plastic bag or rope has been pulled through the tail fin gasket you should check this as soon as possible.

Head for shore and dismantle the propeller there. You can then remove anything that has become entangled and check whether the gasket has been damaged.

Damaged gasket	→	Diagram on the left
Broken shear pin	→	Diagram on the left
Slipping friction clutch	→	Diagram on the left

POWER DECREASES GRADUALLY

Test the spark plugs (see page 16)	→	Workshop
The filter is blocked or there is water in the fuel	→	See diagram on the left
The cooling intake is blocked	→	See page 11
The ignition setting has shifted. Even with smaller engines this is a job for the professional	→	Workshop
Soot encrustment in the engine due to use of wrong or dirty oil or a wrongly tuned carburettor or fuel injection. Sometimes cleaning with an engine cleaning fluid will help, otherwise:	→	Workshop

Other causes:

Fouling of the bottom of the boat	→	Clean it
Piston rings stuck	→	Workshop

▲ **A.** *A fishing line has been pulled through the gasket. The gasket may be damaged and you will need to test it (pressure test).*

B. *Shear pin of a propeller without friction clutch. The shear pin has broken and you will need to replace it.*

C. *Propeller with friction clutch. The impact has forced the propeller to rotate on the compression bush (friction clutch). The propeller can be freely rotated despite being in gear. This is an indication that the bush has been damaged. You should repair or replace the propeller and/or the friction clutch.*

▲ *The fuel filter is a simple container for the filter cartridge. As the fuel runs through it, dirt is filtered from it. These particles accumulate inside the filter cartridge and will eventually block it. This will cause so much resistance that eventually fuel will no longer reach the engine. For this reason you should clean the filter cartridge regularly. You can do this with clean petrol after which the filter can be dried with something like a bicycle pump. Don't do this by blowing with your mouth as moisture particles in your breath could block it again just like water in the fuel. You can recognize a polluted filter by the white slime that has built up on it. You should clean or replace it.*

STATIONARY REVS/CARBURETTOR

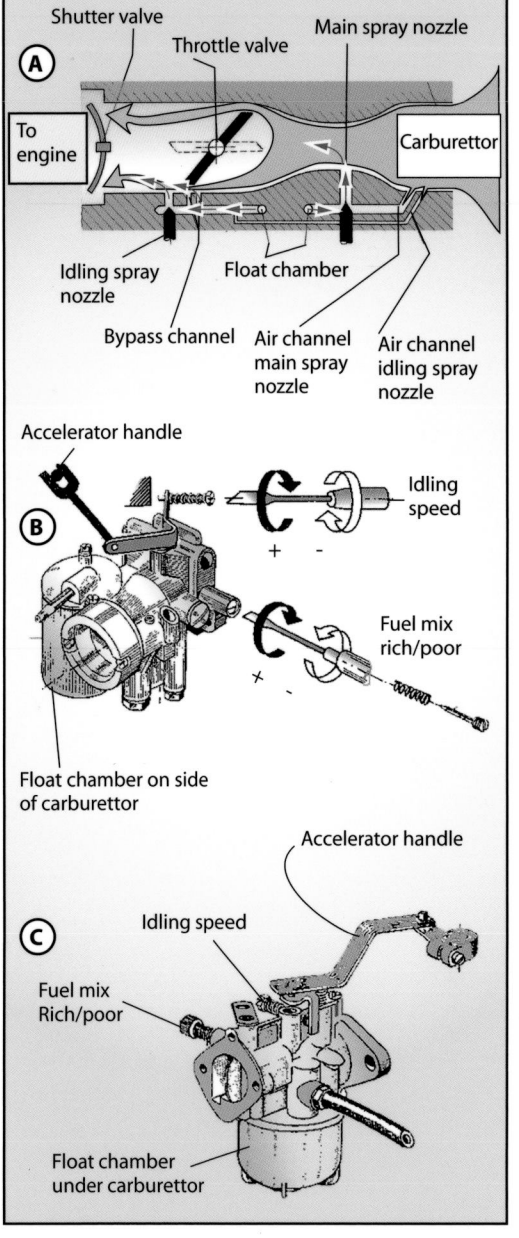

A — Shutter valve, Throttle valve, Main spray nozzle, To engine, Carburettor, Idling spray nozzle, Float chamber, Bypass channel, Air channel main spray nozzle, Air channel idling spray nozzle

B — Accelerator handle, Idling speed, Fuel mix rich/poor, Float chamber on side of carburettor

C — Accelerator handle, Idling speed, Fuel mix Rich/poor, Float chamber under carburettor

BAD TRANSITION FROM STATIONARY TO HIGHER REVS AND/OR NOT ENOUGH REVS WHEN ENGAGED IN FULL THROTTLE

Cause is in the ignition	Test the spark plugs	→ See page 16
	Check the timing	→ Workshop
Cause is in the fuel system	The filter is partly blocked	→ See diagram on page 18
	The fuel pump isn't supplying enough fuel	→ Workshop
	The idling speed is poorly adjusted	→ See drawing on left
Cause is in the engine	The cylinder walls and intake and exit valves are encrusted. Sometimes a lubricant or engine cleaning fluid will help.	
	No result	→ Workshop

◀ If you don't want to study the inner workings of a carburettor, you would be wise to leave its maintenance to a workshop. After having a careful look at the diagrams and text on this page, you will probably understand enough about how it works to be able to adjust its idling speed. Except for in the most modern engines, the carburettor is still the most common method of regulating the air/fuel mix.

From top to bottom the diagrams show:

A construction details and workings, **B** a carburettor with float mounted on the side and **C** a carburettor with float mounted on the bottom.

Top drawing: the throttle valve regulates the amount of fuel (the accelerator). If the throttle valve is shut the main spray nozzle will not deliver any fuel. The air that passes through the remaining slit of the throttle valve sucks fuel from the idling spray nozzle. Extra air is mixed through the bypass channel giving the idling RPM a higher range.

The carburettor can only be adjusted after the engine has warmed up and reached its working temperature. The screw to adjust the idling speed is at the end of the accelerator handle. If you turn the screw clockwise the RPM will increase. This needs to be done carefully. Never adjust the screw more than a quarter turn and wait until the RPM have stabilized. You should adjust the RPM while driving as slowly as possibly and while having the engine running smoothly, or with a rev counter in a test setup.

The second adjustment is the screw which regulates the mix, making it richer or leaner. Set the throttle at idling speed and play with the regulator. Clockwise adjustments make the mixture richer. Turn the screw clockwise and watch how the engine reacts. If the RPM drop and the engine stutters then the mix is too rich. Turn the screw back in the opposite direction. If the mix is too lean the engine will run irregularly and stutter. Find a setting that lets the engine run smoothly. If you are unsuccessful you will have to go to a workshop.

THE TANK LID

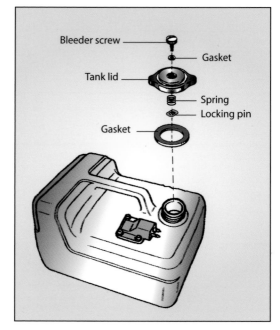

- Bleeder screw
- Gasket
- Tank lid
- Spring
- Locking pin
- Gasket

▲ *One of the most common mistakes is not opening the air vent on the top of the tank. If this happens you will be faced with an engine that suddenly stops after running perfectly for a few minutes. A compressed pump valve is the clearest sign that the fuel is no longer reaching the engine. It's also possible that fuel contaminated with rubber residue has blocked the air vent. You should carefully clean all parts of the tank lid with a cloth soaked in petrol. Watch out for sparks!*

OIL SHORTAGE/PISTON SEIZURE

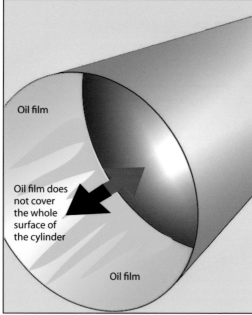

Oil film

Oil film does not cover the whole surface of the cylinder

Oil film

▲ *This is what the inside of the cylinder looks like if the oil film is broken. This happens when there is not enough oil in the petrol. If the engine stops because there isn't enough lubricating oil in the cylinder, there will almost certainly be serious damage to your engine. Unfortunately, you probably won't notice that this is about to happen as you don't usually get any warning before a piston seizes.*

ANALYZING THE MALFUNCTION

ENGINE STALLS AFTER SHORT PERIOD OF RUNNING

Causes with no serious consequences

The fuel system has been checked but the pump valve has been compressed. The tank bleeder has been opened but is blocked. Try to run the engine with the tank filler cap open.

The engine runs! → See diagram on left.

The malfunction is caused by the carburettor → See page 19

Very unusual: The spark plugs have the wrong heat rating. This should never be the case as no one should ever mount the wrong spark plugs in an engine. The correct heat rating can be found in the manual.

Causes with serious consequences

There isn't enough oil in the fuel, the protective oil (two stroke engines) film is missing and the inside of the cylinder may be damaged.

Let the engine cool down and remove the spark plugs. Spray some WD40 into the the spark plug holes. Put the gear into neutral and carefully pull the hand starter. If this is difficult to move or moves irregularly then the engine is probably seriously damaged.

Engine → Workshop

Spark plugs undergo extremely high loads. A spark plug with an incorrect heat rating can lead to major problems in the engine. The spark plugs must handle 30,000 V, a temperature of up to 1,000 degrees Centigrade and a 100 bar pressure, and all of this at a maximum rate of 10,000 revs per second. With the wrong spark plugs the ignition (and therefore the engine) can seriously malfunction. Therefore, when replacing a spark plug, make sure that it has the correct heat rating.

PROPELLER DAMAGE

A slightly bent blade can cause the engine to run irregularly

▲ *While it's unusual for damage to a propeller to be invisible to the human eye yet still create a problem, a slightly bent blade could cause the engine to run irregularly, and you can only really confirm the cause by mounting a spare propeller. The damaged propeller can be repaired in a workshop so you don't need to replace it with a new one. Don't forget to add a little water-resistant grease to the newly-mounted propeller as this makes it easier to remove it again.*

ANALYZING THE MALFUNCTION

ENGINE SMOKES AND RUNS IRREGULARLY

Oil and fuel mix	→	A two stroke engine might be getting too much oil. If the engine has an oil regulator, check it.	
		If the engine doesn't have an oil regulator	→ Workshop
		The tank has not been used for a long time: the oil has sunk to the bottom of the tank and is being sucked into the engine first. Shake the tank vigorously. Remove oily fuel from the piping and filters and check the spark plugs.	→ See page 16
Crankshaft sump	→	The oil return conduit is blocked:	→ Workshop
Exhaust	→	The exhaust leaks (exhaust fumes are being sucked back into the engine). Refasten the exhaust manifold bolts and run the motor for a while without the engine hood on. Replace the engine hood.	
		If the problem recurs, try a new gasket:	→ Workshop

ENGINE RUNS BUT BOAT DOESN'T REACH HULL SPEED

The propeller is lost
→ Mount a spare propeller

Plastic bag in the propeller causing it to spin without any power
→ Clear the propeller → See page 18

The shear pin is broken
→ Replace → See page 18

The friction clutch is broken
→ Mount a spare propeller → See left

BOAT DOESN'T REACH MAXIMUM HULL SPEED (engine suffers from loss of power)

The propeller is bent in such a way that the pitch has changed without causing a major imbalance
→ Mount a spare propeller → See left

The power from the propeller has dropped because a fishing line has got caught
→ Clean the propeller → See page 18

BOAT REACHES HULL SPEED BUT THEN ENGINE REVS INCREASE WITHOUT THE BOAT ACCELERATING

The shear pin has broken (see page 18) or the gears are slipping when accelerating (see page 18).

EMERGENCY START

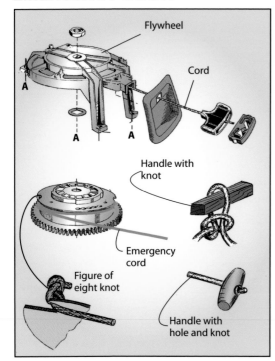

Flywheel

Cord

A

A   A

Handle with knot

Emergency cord

Figure of eight knot

Handle with hole and knot

▲ *It's quite unusual for a starting cord to break or jam. But if it does happen, you can remove the hand starter at the points marked A on the diagram. You can then wind the emergency starter cord around the flywheel and start the engine in this way. It's important to remember that the cord releases itself easily from the flywheel, so use a figure of eight knot. As it isn't tied to your hand, use a handle. When improvising, this is often forgotten! You should always keep a good emergency starter cord in your spare parts box.*

Beware!

Take great care if the engine is running while the hood is off. Hair or clothing can easily be caught by moving parts and this can cause serious injury.

EMERGENCY REPAIRS

ONLY TO BE CARRIED OUT IN EXTREME EMERGENCY!

You can't be towed to safety, so you have to use the engine.

There's no water coming from the tell tale and you cannot find any blockages → Remove the engine hood and feel the temperature of the exhaust manifold. If the temperature is OK, carefully motor onwards. If it's too hot you must immediately switch off the engine and look for the problem.

The engine stops due to a lack of fuel → Check whether fuel can flow from the tank into the hose and priming valve. One of the valves in the priming valve is probably blocked.

The priming valve has been compressed due to low pressure. → Cut the hose either side of the priming valve, and re-connect the hoses with a short piece of piping. Hold the fuel tank above the engine and spray some fuel into the carburettor with an oil spray. Once the engine is running smoothly you can lower the tank again.

The engine is not getting any fuel because a valve is blocked in a fuel connection → Cut away the connection, take the fuel intake hose off the carburettor and attach the hose directly from the fuel tank.

The fuel pump membrane is torn (no spare available) → Dismantle the fuel pump. Dismantle the hose to the filter and attach it directly to the fuel intake on the carburettor. Pump the priming valve. If the engine runs, hold the tank above the engine so gravity forces fuel into the engine. If the engine doesn't run smoothly continue pumping with the priming valve.

Emergency start

Faults in the hand starter are usually related to incorrect use. With most engine types you can wind the emergency starter cord around the flywheel (see diagram on this page). To reach the flywheel you must remove the hand starter. The figure of eight knot of the starting cord is placed in the opening on the edge of the flywheel and the starting cord is wound around the flywheel. You can start the engine by pulling strongly on the cord. The cord must release itself easily from the flywheel and you must never tie it to your hand. Use a handle!

If the hand starter isn't mounted next to the flywheel then you don't have to dismantle it. You may have to remove the flywheel's protective covering.

ADJUSTING STEERING RESISTANCE

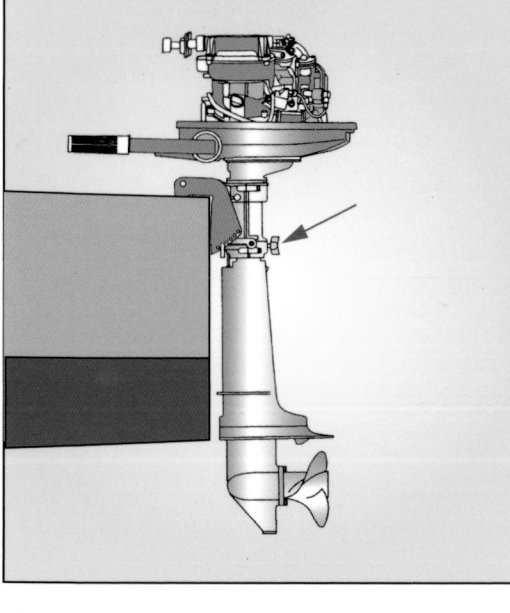

▲ *If there isn't enough steering resistance the engine may vibrate heavily at certain RPM. To minimize this, engines have an adjustable screw on the tail fin. While the engine is running turn the screw clockwise to increase the resistance. Don't adjust the screw by more than a quarter turn.*

Exhaust leakage

If the exhaust leaks, gas will accumulate under the engine hood and get sucked back into the engine through the intake. If the engine hood is removed, fresh air will be drawn in and the engine will run regularly again. Important: check whether all the bolts in the exhaust manifold and in the rest of the exhaust pipe are properly attached. If a seal leaks you should ask a workshop to replace it.

EMERGENCY REPAIRS

WRONG RPM WHILE STATIONARY, OR IRREGULAR RUNNING

Tuning carburettor	→	The idling spray nozzle may be delivering too rich or too lean a mixture.	→ See page 19
	→	The idling screw adjuster is incorrectly tuned.	→ See page 17
Spark plugs	→	The spark plugs are faulty.	→ See page 16
Fuel-oil mix	→	There is too much oil in the petrol; the petrol is of poor quality; the tank has not been used for a long time.	→ Shake the tank
Timing ignition	→	Turning the throttle valve also tunes the ignition. The tuning screw is jammed.	→ Workshop
Exhaust pipe leaks	→	You will only notice this when the engine hood is on.	→ See left

ENGINE RUNS IRREGULARLY AND/OR VIBRATES

It's quite normal for the engine to vibrate while in reverse. While idling, single cylinder engines will always run irregularly and loudly. If this gets worse you should try to find out why.

Engine vibrates more and more while in neutral	→	Engine loose.	→ Secure it more firmly.
Engine vibrates more and more while in gear	→	The propeller is damaged; there is a plastic bag or fishing line etc caught in it. Inspect the propeller and if necessary mount a spare one.	
	→	This will also make it clear whether the problem was caused by the prop. You can't always see damage with the naked eye.	→ Spare prop
	→	Inspect the carburettor. Is the choke fully opened? Is the fuel mix too rich or too lean? Does the float move freely or is the nozzle dirty?	→ See page 17 or visit workshop